WELCOME TO MY COUNTRY

Welcome to
DENMARK

Gareth Stevens Publishing
A WORLD ALMANAC EDUCATION GROUP COMPANY

Written by
KAREN KWEK/CLAYTON TRAPP

Edited by
NAFISAH ISMAIL

Edited in USA by
JIM MEZZANOTTE

Designed by
GEOSLYN LIM

Picture research by
SUSAN JANE MANUEL

First published in North America in 2003 by
Gareth Stevens Publishing
A World Almanac Education Group Company
330 West Olive Street, Suite 100
Milwaukee, Wisconsin 53212 USA

Please visit our web site at:
www.garethstevens.com
For a free color catalog describing
Gareth Stevens Publishing's list of high-quality
books and multimedia programs,
call 1-800-542-2595 (USA) or
1-800-387-3178 (Canada).
Gareth Stevens Publishing's fax: (414) 332-3567.

© **TIMES MEDIA PRIVATE LIMITED 2003**
Originated and designed by
Times Editions
An imprint of Times Media Private Limited
A member of the Times Publishing Group
Times Centre, 1 New Industrial Road
Singapore 536196
http://www.timesone.com.sg/te

Library of Congress Cataloging-in-Publication Data
Kwek, Karen.
Welcome to Denmark / Karen Kwek and Clayton Trapp.
p. cm. — (Welcome to my country)
Contents: Welcome to Denmark! — The land — History —
Government and the economy — People and lifestyle —
Language — Arts — Leisure — Food.
Includes bibliographical references and index.
ISBN 0-8368-2550-0 (lib. bdg.)
1. Denmark—Juvenile literature. [1. Denmark.]
I. Trapp, Clayton. II. Title. III. Series.
DL109.K94   2003
948.9—dc21   2003045740

Printed in Singapore

1 2 3 4 5 6 7 8 9 07 06 05 04 03

PICTURE CREDITS
Art Directors & TRIP Photo Library:
    16 (bottom), 24, 35
Ellen Barone/Houserstock: cover
Hank Barone/Houserstock: 26
Camera Press: 34
Yvette Cardozo: 3 (top), 6 (top)
Danish Tourist Board: 1, 2, 3 (center),
    3 (bottom), 4, 5, 8, 19, 20, 21, 22, 23,
    30, 31 (both), 32, 33, 37, 40, 43, 45
Downtown MoneyPoint: 44 (both)
Focus Team — Italy: 6 (bottom), 27, 28
Getty Images/HultonArchive: 15 (top),
    15 (center), 25
Dave G. Houser: 7, 41
The Hutchison Library: 18
Life File: 9 (bottom)
Royal Danish Embassy: 16 (top)
Scanpix: 9 (top), 29
Topham Picturepoint: 10, 11, 12, 13,
    14, 15 (bottom), 17, 36, 38, 39

Digital Scanning by Superskill Graphics Pte Ltd

Contents

Words that appear in the glossary are printed in **boldface** type the first time they occur in the text.

Welcome to Denmark!

The Kingdom of Denmark is a land of many islands in northern Europe. It was once the center of a mighty **empire**. Today, Denmark is a small, modern country with a rich **culture**. Let's visit Denmark and discover its friendly people and great beauty.

Opposite: This castle is in Copenhagen, the capital of Denmark. It was built by King Christian IV in 1606.

Below: Many Danes begin taking bicycle rides at an early age.

The Flag of Denmark

The Danish flag is called the *Dannebrog* (DAY-nuh-broo). It has a white cross on a red background. The cross represents Denmark's Christian heritage. According to legend, in the thirteenth century, the flag fell from the sky to Danish king Valdemar II on his way to battle.

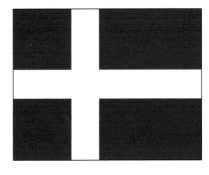

The Land

The Kingdom of Denmark consists of Denmark and two **autonomous** territories, Greenland and the Faroe Islands. Denmark is made up of the Jutland **peninsula** and about five hundred islands. It has an area of 16,639 square miles (43,094 square kilometers). Germany lies south of Denmark. The Skagerrak **Strait** is to the north, the Kattegat and Øresund Straits are to the east, and the North Sea is to the west.

Above:
The Inuit people live in Greenland, a huge, icy island that is northwest of Denmark.

Left:
The Faroe Islands are made up of eighteen islands and a few islets, or tiny islands.

The Jutland peninsula makes up two-thirds of Denmark. The largest and most crowded island is Zealand. Other large islands include Funen, Bornholm, Lolland, and Falster.

Denmark has low hills and flat plains, and it has a lot of rich soil that is good for farming. The highest point in the country, Yding Skovhøj, is only 568 feet (173 meters) high. The country has a long coastline and many **fjords**, or small sea inlets.

Above:
Copenhagen is located on the island of Zealand.

Climate

Denmark has mild weather because of the seas surrounding it and winds that blow in from the west. The average summer temperature is 61° Fahrenheit (16° Celsius), and the average winter temperature is 32° F (0° C). Summer days are extremely long, while winter days are much shorter. Rain falls all year, but the wettest period lasts from about August to December.

Above: Fields of rape, a plant in the mustard family, turn bright yellow during summer on Funen Island.

Plants and Animals

About one-tenth of Denmark's land is covered with forests. Trees that grow in these forests include beech, oak, elm, linden, spruce, and fir. Red deer roam Denmark's forests, and the country is also home to smaller animals, such as foxes, red squirrels, and more than three hundred kinds of birds. The fjords and surrounding seas contain a variety of fish and other sea creatures.

Above: The red squirrel lives in the forests of Denmark.

Left: Red deer are the largest wild animals in Denmark. An adult male can weigh as much as 441 pounds (200 kilograms).

History

About fourteen thousand years ago, **nomads** roamed across Denmark. By A.D. 400, people settled on farms and in villages. In the tenth century, King Gorm of Jutland united Denmark into a single kingdom under his rule.

Vikings, who were skilled sailors and fierce fighters, used Denmark as a base for their attacks on neighboring countries from A.D. 800 to 1050.

Below:
This painting is from a psalter, a type of Christian **manuscript** that was popular in the twelfth century. Christianity grew to be the main religion in Denmark by the end of the tenth century.

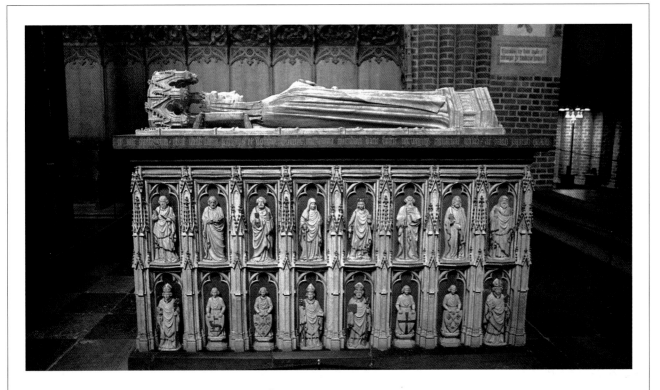

Beginning in the twelfth century, Denmark grew larger and wealthier. In 1380, Denmark and Norway were joined together under Denmark's king Olaf. After Olaf died in 1387, his mother, Margaret I, took his place. In 1397, Sweden joined Denmark and Norway, forming the Kalmar Union. Erik of Pomerania, great-nephew of Margaret I, was crowned king of the union, but Margaret I actually ruled it until her death in 1412. Sweden broke away from the union in 1523.

Above:
Margaret I once ruled Denmark, Norway, and Sweden. She is buried in the cathedral of Roskilde.

Left: The British navy defeated the Danish fleet twice in Copenhagen harbor, once in 1801 and again in 1807.

Wars and Political Changes

From 1543 to 1720, Denmark fought against Sweden in many battles, and by 1660, Denmark had given up a lot of territory to Sweden. In 1807, Denmark sided with France against Britain and other countries in the Napoleonic Wars. When France lost in 1814, Denmark had to give up Norway to Sweden.

In 1849, Denmark established its first democratic **constitution**, which protected the rights of the people and required the king or queen to share power with an elected **parliament**.

In the late 1800s, many improvements were made in education, politics, and other areas of Danish life. In the early twentieth century, these improvements continued. Denmark did not fight in World War I (1914–1918), but after the war, the Danish economy became weak, and many people lost their jobs.

The Danish government tried to stay out of World War II (1939–1945), but German forces **occupied** Denmark from 1940 to the end of the war.

Below: These Danish women are celebrating the end of German occupation in 1945.

Modern Problems

After World War II, Danish leaders tried to improve the economy. By the mid-1970s, Denmark still struggled with many economic problems. The Danish government continues to work on the problems of rising prices and unemployment. Denmark belongs to the European Union (EU) but has not changed its **currency** to the euro, which is used by other EU countries.

Below: Poul Nyrup Rasmussen was the prime minister of Denmark from 1993 to 2001. He is a strong supporter of the EU.

King Christian IV (1577–1648)

Christian IV was king of Denmark and Norway from 1588 to 1648. During his rule, trade and shipping **flourished**, and new cities were built. He is considered one of Denmark's greatest rulers.

King Christian IV

Queen Margaret I (1353–1412)

Margaret I of Denmark married Norwegian king Haakon VI when she was only ten years old. After the deaths of her husband and then her son, King Olaf, Margaret ruled Denmark and Norway. A skilled leader, she also gained control of Sweden, forming the Kalmar Union.

Queen Margaret I

Thorvald Stauning (1873–1942)

Thorvald Stauning became a member of the Danish parliament in 1898. He introduced many laws that improved the Danish economy and the quality of life for the Danish people.

Thorvald Stauning

Government and the Economy

Denmark is a constitutional monarchy. The power to make laws is shared by a **monarch** and a parliament, known as the *Folketing* (FULL-guh-ting). The Folketing has 179 members, including two members from Greenland and two members from the Faroe Islands. The monarch appoints the prime minister. Although the monarch is the head of state, the prime minister actually runs

Above: Margrethe II has been queen of Denmark since 1972.

the country with help from a cabinet. The cabinet is made up of twenty ministers. The ministers are in charge of various government departments, including the departments of justice, finance, and agriculture.

Denmark is divided into fourteen regions called counties. Each county is governed by a county council that is elected every four years. The councils each choose a county mayor.

Above: Members of the Folketing meet regularly to discuss national issues.

Opposite: The Copenhagen Town Hall was built between 1892 and 1905.

Economy

Farming used to be an important part of Denmark's economy, and almost two-thirds of the country's land is still used to grow crops. Today, however, most of the economy is made up of service industries, manufacturing, and trade. Service industries include health care and education. Manufacturing industries include construction, food processing, and **textiles**. Denmark also has a strong fishing industry.

Above: This man is working at a factory in Copenhagen. Although farms in Denmark still grow many crops, including wheat and potatoes, only 4 percent of the population now works in agriculture.

Transportation

Denmark's economy is helped by a modern and efficient transportation system. Roads and railways link cities and towns, while ferries connect the Danish islands with the mainland and with each other. Copenhagen is the transportation hub of Denmark. The country's largest seaport is located in Copenhagen and so is the main airport, Kastrup Airport. Together with Norway and Sweden, Denmark owns Scandinavian Airlines.

Left:
Opened on July 1, 2000, the Øresund Bridge crosses the Øresund Strait to connect the city of Copenhagen with the city of Malmö, Sweden.

People and Lifestyle

The Kingdom of Denmark includes people with Danish, German, Inuit, and Faroese backgrounds. Most of the people in Denmark are Danish, but some Germans live in southern Jutland. Greenland is home to the Inuit people and people with Inuit and European **ancestors**. Most Faroese are descended from Vikings who lived on the Faroe Islands in the ninth century.

Below: Many Danes, such as these children from Jutland, have blond hair and blue eyes. In addition to Danes, Denmark is also home to **immigrants** from Africa, Eastern Europe, and the Middle East.

City and Countryside

Most Danish people live in apartments or small houses in or near cities and towns. Some city dwellers also build houses outside of the city so they can enjoy a break from city living.

People who live in the countryside usually run small farms, growing crops or raising livestock. Most houses in the countryside have modern features such as electricity and telephones.

Above: This Danish couple is taking a walk along one of Copenhagen's main streets. Over one-quarter of the population of Denmark lives in Copenhagen. Other large cities include Odense, Århus, and Ålborg.

Families

Danish people value family life. Family members spend a lot of time together, and families often gather to celebrate holidays and special occasions, such as birthdays, baptisms, and weddings.

Most Danish families include only one or two children, and children may live with their parents until they reach their mid-twenties. Often, both parents work outside the home, and all family members share household duties.

Quality of Life

The people of Denmark enjoy a high standard of living. The government offers many social services, including free medical care, and Danish people often live to a very old age. Danish women lead independent lives. Many women are well educated, and they make up more than half the workforce. The government has opened child care centers to make it easier for women to work outside the home.

Below: Danish women now hold many different jobs, including positions in the armed forces and the government. These women are involved with a large business conference in Copenhagen.

Education

Between the ages of seven and sixteen, all children in Denmark must attend *folkeskole* (FULL-guh-skool), which is the country's elementary and middle school. Some students attend private schools, but the majority of students attend public schools. Students study a variety of subjects, including Danish, mathematics, science, history, religion, and geography. Beginning in grade five, they also have to learn English.

Below:
A kindergarten teacher in the city of Ålborg reads a story to her students. Many children in Denmark attend preschool or kindergarten between the ages of five and six.

After folkeskole, some students attend schools that provide training in a **vocation**. Other students move on to high school, called *gymnasium* (gim-NAY-shee-yoom), which lasts three years and prepares students for higher education at a university.

Denmark has fifteen universities. The oldest of them, the University of Copenhagen, was founded in 1479. Some universities specialize in certain fields, such as architecture, art, or engineering. Denmark also has folk high schools, which offer adults a variety of classes in general subjects.

Religion

Since the tenth century, most Danish people have been Christians. Today, about 95 percent of the population of Denmark belongs to a **Protestant** faith known as Evangelical Lutheranism. The Evangelical Lutheran Church is the official church of Denmark and is headed by the Danish monarch. Only a small percentage of Danes attend church services on a regular basis.

Above:
Frederikskirke, or the Marble Church, in Copenhagen, was inspired by St. Peter's Church in Rome, Italy. The church is one of the city's famous landmarks.

Until the sixteenth century, Roman Catholicism was the official religion of Denmark, and today it is the country's second largest faith. Other Christian faiths in Denmark include the Danish Baptist Church, the Methodist Church, and the Anglican Church. Denmark is also home to Seventh Day Adventists, Jehovah's Witnesses, and Mormons.

Only a small number of people in Denmark practice non-Christian faiths, such as Judaism, Hinduism, and Islam.

Below:
Many churches in Denmark, such as this one in the city of Ribe, have high, arched ceilings.

Language

Denmark's official language is Danish, which is similar to Norwegian, Swedish, and Icelandic. In southern Jutland, some people prefer to use German. People in Greenland speak Greenlandic, an Inuit language that includes Danish words, and people on the Faroe Islands speak Faroese, which is similar in some ways to Danish. Many Danish people also speak English.

Below: People in Denmark read a wide variety of newspapers, which are sold throughout the country.

Literature

Hans Christian Andersen (1805–1875) is one of the most famous writers from Denmark. Andersen wrote *The Ugly Duckling, The Emperor's New Clothes,* and other fairy tales. Ludvig Holberg (1684–1754), considered the father of Danish literature, wrote funny poems and plays. Today, important Danish writers include poet Marianne Larsen (1942–) and Vita Andersen (1944–), author of poems and short stories.

Arts

Music

Carl August Nielsen (1865–1931) is a well-known Danish composer. Victor Borge (1909–2000), another Dane, blended classical music and comedy.

Danish people enjoy many styles of music from traditional folk tunes to pop and rock songs. Two top Danish bands are Aqua and Kashmir.

Left: Jazz came to Denmark in the 1920s. Now, it is very popular. These musicians are performing on a riverboat as part of the Copenhagen Jazz Festival, which is held each summer.

Painting and Sculpture

Early Danish painters worked mainly on **portraits**. One of the first artists to paint scenes of everyday life was Christoffer Wilhelm Eckersberg (1783–1853). Asger Jorn (1914–1973) was one of the most important Danish artists of the twentieth century. Denmark's greatest sculptor is Bertel Thorvaldsen (1770–1844). More recently, Robert Jacobsen (1912–1993) earned fame for his iron sculptures.

Performing Arts

The performing arts in Denmark are excellent. Opened in 1748, the Royal Theater in Copenhagen is home to the Danish royal theater, opera, and ballet companies. Danish theater performs a wide variety of plays, and opera draws many fans. The Royal Danish Ballet, established in the 1700s, is famous around the world.

Above: These performers at Den Fynske Landsby, an open-air museum in Odense, are acting in a play based on a fairy tale by Hans Christian Andersen.

Design and Architecture

Danish design is admired around the world. Craft companies in Denmark produce beautiful silverware, silver jewelry, ceramics, and **porcelain**. The architect Arne Jacobsen (1902–1971) became famous for creating buildings that were simple in design, and he was also well-known for his furniture. Jørn Utzon (1918–) designed the famous Sydney Opera House in Australia.

Left:
The Egg Chair was created by architect Arne Jacobsen. Many designers have copied its smooth, simple look.

Leisure

People in Denmark enjoy the outdoors. Walking is especially popular. Many families go for walks on the weekends, taking advantage of the country's many nature trails and walking paths. People also enjoy cycling. Denmark is mostly flat, and it has a lot of **scenic** bicycle paths. Other popular outdoor activities include hunting, fishing, and visiting the country's sandy beaches.

Left: Cycling is a popular hobby in Denmark and a great way to get around. Most of Denmark's roads have separate cycling paths.

Left:
Opened in 1843, Tivoli Gardens in Copenhagen offers many attractions, including rides, circus acts, and fireworks displays.

Beautiful Parks

Denmark has many beautiful parks and public gardens. Some of these parks and gardens surround castles, palaces, and grand old houses that are open to the public.

Indoor Fun

Danish people enjoy reading books, watching television, and playing card games. They also enjoy playing chess. The Danish chess player Brent Larsen has won several international chess tournaments.

Sports

Danes love sports. They spend much of their free time either playing or watching one of the many sports they enjoy. Denmark's most popular sport is soccer. The country's national team won the European Cup in 1992, and Danish soccer players are among the best in the world. Danish people of all ages enjoy handball, badminton, gymnastics, tennis, and cycling. Golf has also become popular in Denmark.

Above: France's Marcel Desailly (*right*) fights for control of the ball with Denmark's Brian Laudrup during a 1998 World Cup match. Besides Brian Laudrup, other top soccer players from Denmark include Michael Laudrup, Peter Schmeichel, and Thomas Sørensen.

Water sports are also popular in Denmark. Many Danes sail in their free time. They also enjoy swimming, diving, canoeing, and windsurfing.

Olympic Gold

Denmark's athletes have won many Olympic gold medals. The winners include yachtsman Paul Elvstrøm in 1948, 1952, 1956, and 1960, and badminton player Poul Erik Høyer in 1996. In 1996 and 2000, the women's handball team earned the gold medals.

Below: Denmark's many rivers and lakes are perfect for water sports, such as canoeing.

Holidays and Festivals

Christmas, or *jul* (YOOL), is one of Denmark's most important holidays. Christmas celebrations last almost a month, beginning on the first day of December. On Christmas Eve, Danish families decorate a tree and sit down to a traditional dinner. Christmas Day is spent with relatives and friends.

Midsummer's Eve, on June 23, is a popular festival. On this night, people gather around huge bonfires, and they make speeches and sing.

Left:
Danish families in Copenhagen gather around a bonfire on Midsummer's Eve.

Public Holidays

Liberation Day, on May 5, marks the day in 1945 when Denmark was freed from German occupation at the end of World War II. On the night before the holiday, people put candles in their windows. Denmark also celebrates two half-day holidays: Worker's Day on May 1, and Constitution Day on June 5. Constitution Day honors the day, in 1849, when King Frederik VII signed Denmark's first constitution.

Above:
People celebrate Liberation Day with parades all over the country. Danes also mark a U.S. holiday, Independence Day on July 4.

Food

The Danish diet includes meat, fish, cheese, and bread. Most Danes eat breakfast, lunch, dinner, and a late supper. Breakfast is usually cereal and *morgenbrød* (MWARN-brohd), which is bread and rolls, served with cheese, jam, and, sometimes, eggs. For lunch and the late supper, Danes often serve open-faced sandwiches, but they prepare a bigger, hot meal for dinner.

Left:
The *smørrebrød* (SMUHR-brohd), an open-faced sandwich, can be made with many different kinds of ingredients and is a favorite for lunch and late supper.

40

Left:
Many restaurants in Copenhagen serve traditional Danish dishes.

Traditional Favorites

Most Danish people love to eat meat, and the most popular meat is pork. Meat dishes are often served with potatoes and pickled beets. Danes also eat a lot of fish, such as salmon, cod, mackerel, and herring. Denmark is known for its cheeses, especially a mild, creamy cheese called Havarti. The most traditional Danish dish is roast duckling stuffed with apples and prunes. Danes also enjoy sweet pastries and cakes with rich fillings.

DENMARK

Faroe Islands

NORTH ATLANTIC OCEAN

Greenland

Arctic Circle

	National Boundary
	County Boundary
■	Capital
●	City
～	River

N

Skagerrak Strait

SWEDEN

● Ålborg

Kattegat Strait

NORDJYLLAND

Randers

VIBORG

Gudenå

ÅRHUS

Jutland

RINGKØBING

Århus ●

Yding Skovhøj
(568 ft/173 m)

Øresund Strait

Lake Arresø

FREDERIKSBORG

KØBENHAVN
■ COPENHAGEN

RIBE

VEJLE

Roskilde ●

Zealand

ROSKILDE

Ribe ●

NORTH

SEA

Odense ●

Funen

FYN

VESTSJÆLLAND

BORNHOL

SØNDERJYLLAND

STORSTRØM

BALTIC

Lolland

Falster

SEA

G E R M A N Y

42

Above: Egeskov Castle has stood for hundreds of years on Funen Island.

Ålborg B2
Århus (city) B3
Århus (county)
    A3–B4

Baltic Sea D3–D5
Bornholm (county) D4

Copenhagen C4

Falster Island C5
Faroe Islands A1–A2
Frederiksborg
    (county) C3–C4
Funen Island B4
Fyn (county) B4–B5

Germany A5–D5
Greenland B1–B2
Gudenå River B3–A4

Jutland (region) A2–B4

Kattegat Strait B2–C3
København
    (county) C4

Lake Arresø C4
Lolland Island B5–C5

Nordjylland (county)
    A2–B3
North Atlantic Ocean
    B1–B2
North Sea A3–A5

Odense B4
Øresund Strait C3–C4

Randers B3
Ribe (city) A4
Ribe (county) A4

Ringkøbing (county)
    A3–A4
Roskilde (city) C4
Roskilde (county) C4

Skagerrak Strait A2
Sønderjylland
    (county) A4–B5
Storstrøm (county)
    B5–C4
Sweden B1–D4

Vejle (county)
    A3–B4
Vestsjælland
    (county) B4–C4
Viborg (county)
    A2–B3

Yding Skovhøj B3

Zealand Island
    B4–C4

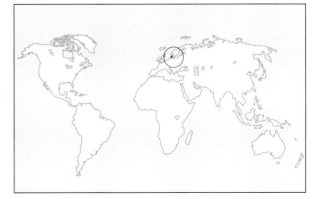

Quick Facts

Official Name	Kingdom of Denmark
Capital	Copenhagen
Main Languages	Danish, Faroese, Greenlandic
Population	5,368,854 (July 2002 estimate)
Land Area	16,639 square miles (43,094 square km)
Counties	Århus, Bornholm, Frederiksborg, Fyn, København, Nordjylland, Ribe, Ringkøbing, Roskilde, Sønderjylland, Storstrøm, Vejle, Vestsjælland, Viborg
Highest Point	Yding Skovhøj 568 feet (173 m)
Major River	Gudenå
Major Lake	Lake Arresø
Main Religion	Evangelical Lutheranism
Major Cities	Ålborg, Århus, Copenhagen, Odense, Roskilde
Major Holidays	Easter (March/April), Liberation Day (May 5), Constitution Day (June 5), Christmas (December 25)
Currency	Danish Krone (6.88 DKK = U.S. $1 as of 2003)

Opposite: Tours along Copenhagen's harbor and canals are a popular way to see the sights and sounds of the country's capital city.

Glossary

ancestors: the members of families who lived in earlier times; past generations.

autonomous: self-governing.

constitution: a set of laws that establish how a country is governed.

culture: the customs, beliefs, language, literature, and art of a particular people or country.

currency: the money used by a certain country or countries.

***Dannebrog*:** the Danish name for the flag of Denmark, which means "Danish cloth" in Danish.

empire: a group of countries or territories that are all ruled by the same government.

fjords: narrow sea inlets, usually between cliffs or steep hills.

flourished: grew to be strong, healthy, and successful.

immigrants: people who move from their home countries to settle in another country.

manuscript: a book or collection of papers with words that have been written by hand or typed instead of printed by a printing press.

monarch: a king or queen.

nomads: people who have no permanent home and move from place to place, often when the seasons change.

occupied: taken over or captured by another country's armed forces.

parliament: a group of government representatives who are elected by the people to make a country's laws.

peninsula: a long strip of land that is surrounded by water on three sides.

porcelain: a particular kind of ceramic that is very hard and usually white.

portraits: pictures of people that are often just of the face and show the people posing a certain way.

Protestant: part of a particular group of Christian faiths that differ from Roman Catholicism.

scenic: having beautiful views.

strait: a narrow channel of water that connects larger bodies of water.

textiles: fabrics, such as clothing.

vocation: a profession or a specialized kind of work in which a person is, or hopes to be, employed.

More Books to Read

Denmark. Countries of the World series. Patrick J. Murphy (Capstone Press)

Denmark in Pictures. Visual Geography series. (Lerner)

Favorite Fairy Tales Told in Denmark. Virginia Haviland (Beech Tree)

Grandchildren of the Vikings. Matti A. Pitkanen (Lerner)

Hans Christian Andersen: Denmark's Famous Author. Anna Carew-Miller (Mason Crest)

The Raven's Gift: A True Story from Greenland. Kelly Dupre (Houghton Mifflin)

The Vikings: 350 Years of Adventure to Unlock and Discover. Treasure Chests series. Fiona MacDonald (Running Press)

The Viking News. History News series. Rachel Wright (Gareth Stevens)

The Yellow Star: The Legend of King Christian X of Denmark. Carmen Agra Deedy (Peachtree Publishers)

Videos

Hans Christian Andersen: My Life as a Fairytale. (Artisan Home Entertainment)

Iceland and Greenland. Globe Trekker series. (555 Productions)

Scandinavia: Denmark, Sweden and Norway. Travel the World series. (Questar)

The Vikings. Explorers of the World series. (Schlessinger Media)

Web Sites

www.leapingmatch.com/en

www.lego.com

www.mnh.si.edu/vikings/start.html

www.puffin.fo/travel/gallery/galindex.html

Due to the dynamic nature of the Internet, some web sites stay current longer than others. To find additional web sites, use a reliable search engine with one or more of the following keywords to help you locate information about Denmark. Keywords: *Copenhagen, Faroe Islands, Greenland, Kalmar Union,* The Little Mermaid.

Index